Resolutions

*Finding the Answers
We Spend a Lifetime Searching For*

C.J. Marie

Dedicated to all my friends and family
who are searching for peace in their lives
and joy in their hearts.

Books by C.J. Marie

Timeless Elegance

Resolutions

Revelations

Reflections

Words of Wisdom

Accents of a Women

Captured Thoughts

Afterthoughts of Yesterday

Legacy of Stable Dreams

Shadowed Love

Reflections of Time

Melody of Love

Days of Difference

Children's Stories:

Mi Primer Dia-Escolar

My First Day in Kindergarten

Chap Books:

Of Love and Sorrow

Fly With Your Dreams

Guides:

Tell Me What to Do

Pageant Tips

Table of Contents

A Season of Change

The seasons of change in our lives transform with each passing decade. Our transitions are shaped by our thoughts, values, and beliefs, and can be observed as various phases of life. With a positive mindset, you can face life's challenges with confidence. Resilience is key to overcoming adversity. Rising above any problem that comes your way requires great courage and perseverance.

We are all here to learn life lessons. As we paint the canvas of our lives, these seasons teach us to press forward with hope. The seasons of our lives are transitions and each one holds its own subtle beauty.

Enjoy each decade and be grateful for the privilege of living. Live in the moment and capture the joyful feelings that come with it.

The Eddy Tree

As I gaze at the wavy waters of the East River under the Hell-gate bridge in Astoria, Queens N.Y., my mind takes me back to a time of innocence when love and exploration went hand in hand. It is comforting to remember the beautiful Astoria Park and the tree carved with the name Eddy. My teenage love and I would park the car under a moonlit sky and speak the language of love so eloquently. Little did we know back then that this memory would mark the beginning of a lifelong friendship.

Those moonlit skies, reflecting on the shimmering river, glistened beautifully over the waters. Many years have passed since then, and so much has changed. Yet, even though my teenage friend and I have gone our separate ways, we still remain more than good friends-more like family. It was a chapter in my book of days that paved the way for my future. So many emotions, pains, and joys have transpired throughout the years. Death and the loss of loved ones are just a few of the events most of us face in our lifetime. Life is not easy, but through it all, there are countless blessings. Good people have entered my life, offering support during difficult times.

There have been so many changes and emotions, too many to write about. Confusion still clouds my mind at times, and as I age, the reality of life becomes more apparent. I was young when I first experienced the loss of loved ones in my family, so my own mortality felt like a distant thought.

Now, as I approach my golden years and witness the aging process in myself and those around me, it becomes reality. Age is age; There is no denying it. One thing is certain: you cannot reclaim your youth, but you can remain young at heart. In this last chapter of my book of days, I embrace freedom of choice. I am accountable only to myself and to God. I strive to live life to the fullest, with passion, purpose, gratitude, and love. I cherish the many blessings that surround me.

Do not stand at my grave and weep

I am not there. I do not sleep.

I am a thousand winds that blow.

I am the diamond glints on snow.

I am the sunlight on ripened grain.

I am the gentle autumn rain.

When you awaken in the mornings hush,
I am the swift uplifting rush

of quiet birds encircled flight.

I am the soft stars that shine at night.

Do not stand at my grave and cry;

I am not there. I did not die.

— Mary Elizabeth Frye

◆

I think the hardest part of loving someone
is having to say goodbye rather learning to live without them.
Always trying to fill the void,
the emptiness that's left inside your heart when they go

◆

Let your faith always be better than your fear

Don't look back with regret, look forward with hope

It's your road and you are alone. Others may walk it with you, but no one can walk it for you

— Rumi

The key to happiness is knowing you have the power of choosing what to accept and what to let go

— Nick Vecchio

Sometimes we don't realize the blessings we have until we no longer have them.
Appreciate all the blessings in your life,
take none for granted

— Catherine Pulsifer

I love hearing old songs I used to love.
They are like memories you can always go back to

♦

There is always a blessing to be grateful for

– C.J. Marie

♦

The home we are looking for in this world
is within us all along.
The lost home that we are seeking is ourselves,
it is the story we carry in our soul

– Michael Meade

Five Daily Reminders:

1, You cannot change your past

2. Others' opinions do not define reality

3. Positive thoughts cultivate positive actions

4. Overthinking a problem will not solve a problem

5. You cannot make everyone happy

– Lessons Taught by Life

♦

As I watched my mother slip away from life,
it reminded me of a beautiful flower
slowly wilting away, day by day

– C. J. Marie

Sometimes you have to eat your words,
check your ego, swallow your pride,
and accept that you are wrong.
It's not giving up, it's called growing up

– Lessons Taught by Life

Be the things you love most about the people who are gone

There are some situations that no longer deserve your time,
energy, and forces you to make good choices

Sometimes the lonely path is the only path where
you learn more about yourself
and most importantly find your inner peace

– Roger Lee Quotes

Some days I wish I could go back in life.
Not to change anything,
but feel a few things twice

I regret nothing in my life,
even if my past was full of hurt.
I still look back and smile,
because it made me who I am today

Learn from the past, live in the now,
and be optimistic about the future

The reason I'm old and wise is because God protected me when I was young and stupid

◆

A wonderful person finds amazing beauty in everything and everyone

– Debasish Mridha

◆

The Desire Factor

Desire is defined as a strong feeling of wanting to attain something beyond what you currently have. It is the driving force that motivates you to strive for more, whether it's more money, prestige, or recognition. Desire can mean something different to each person, but how strong your desires are will ultimately determine your success in achieving your goals.

For instance, if you desire something deeply enough, you will do whatever it takes to make it happen. You must think outside the box and approach things differently. Thinking this way allows you to stand out from the ordinary and be recognized for your unique qualities. These are the key strategies for winning in the fame of life. Desire is the motivation and catalyst for reaching your dreams; without it, your dreams remain nothing more than wishes of the heart.

Sometimes you have to let go of the picture
of what you thought life would be like
and learn to find joy in the story
you are actually living

— Rachel Marie Martin

◆

I don't know how my story will end,
but nowhere in my text will it every read that I gave up

◆

Life has its challenges and time changes people,
friendships and relationships can become difficult;
there is always something to take away
from every experience we face in any situation.
Remember people come into our lives for a reason,
a season, or a lifetime.

◆

Random Thoughts

There are moments when my mind drifts, transporting me to another place and time. It can be difficult to cope with the emotions of the past. At random times, vivid flashes of places appear in my mind, allowing me to walk through those moments as if they were happening again. These memories are so clear that they stir intense physical and emotional reactions, my heart races, a sense of suffocation takes hold, and sweat trickles down my forehead.

I asked myself, why do I let these feelings overwhelm me? Why does my mind torment me without warning? It feels as though I have no control over my senses. How can I find my way out of this confusing state? These recurring scenarios haunt me, when past images keep playing over and over again.

I wonder why they persist. Is it because I missed my past so deeply? I cherish those old days and longed for the loved ones who are no longer with me. Perhaps it's all connected. Someday, I hope to find the answers to these questions and make peace with these lingering memories.

*Don't wait for things to get easier, simpler, better. Life
will always be complicated, learn to be happy right now.
Otherwise, you'll run out of time*

◆

*It's not the things we get,
but the hearts we touch
that will measure our success in life*

◆

*Live like there is no tomorrow,
love like you are on borrowed time*

◆

Your past milestones are meant to guide you, not define you

◆

Some things have to end, so better things to begin

◆

*We live within borrowed time and walk in rented shoes.
If we fade, we fade!
But let us have loved, laughed, and forgiven*

◆

You are the beautiful memory I keep locked in my heart

— Narwin Grewal

Memories are always pressed between the pages of our minds

— C.J. Marie

There comes a day when you realize turning the page
is the best feeling in the world,
because you realize there's so much more to the book
than the pages you were stuck on

— Zayn Malik

Next time you're stuck, take a step back, inhale and laugh.
Remember who you are and why you are here.
You are never given anything in this world
that you can't handle.
Be strong, be flexible, love yourself, and love others.
Always remember just keep moving forward

Maybe one day we'll finally understand. Until then, I hope you live your best life and I hope you really do all the things you always wanted to do

♦

Live Your Dreams

What is a dream keeper? It's someone who keeps their dreams to themselves. Harboring your dreams while filling them with thoughts of failure will only lead to inaction. As the years pass, regret sets in. Excuses become the justification for why your dreams never came to fruition. Money, fear, lack of knowledge, and the hesitation to take risks are what hold dream keepers back from moving forward.

Where are the dream keepers? Where are the visionaries? Following your dreams can lead you down a path you never thought possible.

Don't sabotage yourself. Take the chance, life is filled with opportunities you never imagined. Take the plunge and strive to conquer your dreams. My motto is: "Dreams without action remain just wishes and daydreams".

*An apology doesn't mean that you're wrong
and the other person is right.
It just means that the value of your relationship
is more important than your own ego*

– Emrich Maria Romagna

*At the end of the day people won't remember what you said
or did, they will remember how you made them feel*

*When the elderly die a library is lost and volumes of wisdom
and knowledge are gone*

– African Proverb

*Making someone feel good about themselves and allowing
them to see how important they are is a gift you give yourself*

– C.J. Marie

One day I will be just a memory

Don't worry about getting old, worry about thinking old

◆

Moments become memories and people become lessons in life

◆

Sometimes the things we can't change end up changing us

◆

Life's biggest tragedy is
that we get old too soon and wise too late

— Benjamin Franklin

Chance

Take the chance. Life is full of opportunities you never imagined possible. Embrace the plunge and challenge yourself. Never let fear hold you back from trying.

Strive to achieve your dreams, no matter how long it takes. As I always say, "dreams without action remain nothing more than wishes and daydreams"

Don't be disappointed if people refuse to help you. Remember the words of Einstein: "I am thankful to all those who said no. Because of them I did it myself"

When you have more years behind you then in the front of you, you think differently. Live in the moment and don't worry about tomorrow

– C.J. Marie

Even though your wound is healed, the scar remains always to be remembered

– C.J. Marie

If you want to speak to an intelligent person, speak to yourself

– George Katz

In the final analysis it is between you and God,
it was never between you and them anyway

— Mother Teresa

It's hard to forget someone
who gave you so much to remember

It's hard to turn the page
when you know someone won't be in the next chapter,
but the story must go on

— Thomas Wilder

There are friends, there is family,
and then there are those rare friends who become
family for life

There is Magic in Thinking

O ur brain is magical. It allows us to think, feel, generate ideas, and form attitudes and emotions. Many of us live in the realm of imagination, envisioning what should or could be. The question is: do you live your life to its greatest potential? Many would probably answer, no. Life itself is a challenge, but through struggle, it can become extraordinary.

So many ideas remain frozen in our minds, paralyzed by the fear of failure. However, there is no true failure in life, experience is both a lesson and a form of magic. People make things happen, and when ideas are set in motion, they soar, reaching new heights.

Live your dream through the magic of your thinking.

*Sometimes our lives have to be completely shaken up,
changed, and rearranged to relocate us to a place
we're meant to be*

*Often when you think you're at the end of something,
you're at the beginning of something else*

– Fred Rogers

*Walk by faith not by sight,
and let his word be your guiding light*

– 2 Corinthians 5:7

*Remember when you forgive, you heal.
And when you let go, you grow*

*Sometimes things on the outside look better
than the things that are going on inside*

– C.J. Marie

Inside My Closet

My closet holds many memories. How is that possible, you may ask? Each item of clothing is sentimental, as most pieces carry a memory with them. My closet contains clothes from decades ago, and fortunately, my size has never changed. As I handle and look at each piece, happy and sad memories flood my mind.

There's the blue pantsuit I wore on 9/11, a day no one will ever forget. It's etched in my mind. As a teacher, I remember vividly trying to keep my class calm while we waited for our parents to pick them up. There's a blouse I kept from my son's first birthday, and the same one I wore the day I had my hair and nails done for his wedding.

Crazy as it seems, I am very nostalgic. I even have college clothes from the 70s, which I recently wore to a 70s party. People ask where I got my outfit from, and I told them they were original pieces from many decades ago. I also have clothes and costumes that my mom made for me before she passed, and I treasure them deeply.

These are just a few items; There are many more. When I immerse myself in these long-ago memories, they touched my heart. These memories are precious to me. They take me back to another place and time that I never want to forget good or bad, they are sacred to me. Perhaps that is what makes me unique in my own way.

Loving What Is

hat does it mean to love what is? It means to accept what we cannot change. This is a question many of us ask ourselves, and in life, we are often faced with choices. Our lives are shaped by the decisions we make. While some situations are beyond our control, there are many things we can choose to change.

If you choose to love what it is, you've made a conscious or unconscious decision that is not worth the time or energy to take the chance and pursue something different. However, there is another perspective to consider to love what is and to have gratitude. Many people settle for the status quo, surrendering to it. If you have made peace with that mindset, then you have found your happiness.

There are others who adopt the mindset of, it is what it is. For some, it's difficult to step outside of their comfort zone and follow a different path. Keep in mind that there is no right or wrong way of thinking; We are all different in our thoughts and perceptions. We each make our own individual choices.

They say, life is what you make it. If you want to change your life significantly, you must choose to do so with courage and hope.

*If you live in the past, it will destroy your future. Live for
what today has to offer not what yesterday has taken away*

*Life humbles you. As you grow older,
you stop chasing the big things
and start valuing the little things.
Alone time, long walks, and quality time with loved ones.
Simplicity becomes the ultimate goal*

◆

*As years go by,
we realize that memories are perhaps the greatest
and most priceless treasures
one can possibly possess*

– Narwin Grewal

◆

*As long as we have memories, yesterday remains
As long as we have hope, tomorrow waits
As long as we have love, today is beautiful*

◆

Rules of Life

1. Be kind
2. Listen more, speak less
3. Speak the truth gently
4. Apologize when needed
5. Never stop learning
6. Help without expecting returns
7. Value your time
8. Stay curious
9. Celebrate small wins
10. Avoid comparisons
11. Spend time in nature
12. Forgive others – and yourself
13. Exercise regularly
14. Eat well
15. Drink water
16. Smile often
17. Save for rainy days
18. Sleep enough
19. Live in the moment
20. Respect boundaries
21. Be grateful daily
22. Speak less; do more

My Golden Years

As I approach my golden years and observe the aging process in myself and those around me, its reality becomes undeniable. Change is inevitable, and there is no turning back the clock. One thing is certain, though you can't reclaim your youth, but you can remain young at heart.

In this final chapter of my journey, I embrace the freedom of choice, accountable only to myself and to God. I strive to live my life to the fullest, with purpose, gratitude, and love, cherishing the many blessings that life has bestowed upon me.

Author's Note

Resolutions is the third book in the **Trilogy of Timeless Wisdom** series. It contains thought-provoking quotes designed to stimulate the mind and reveal the inner thoughts of self-discovery. By allowing us to gain a crystal-clear vision, the solutions presented in this book lead to conclusions that shape the life we live today.

This book aims to inspire individuals to live the life they choose, in a peaceful and constructive way. It offers a path for transition and encourages the resolutions we make within ourselves to create a better life.

The Trilogy of Timeless Wisdom

by C.J. Marie

Each of us carries stories, lessons, and moments that shape who we become. Through *Reflections, Revelations,* and *Resolutions,* C.J. Marie invites readers on a heartfelt journey toward self-discovery, gratitude, and renewal.

Together, these three volumes form **The Trilogy of Timeless Wisdom** – a celebration of life's beauty, faith, and resilience. Each book stands alone as a companion for the soul, yet together they form a complete portrait of inspiration that uplifts the heart and quiets the spirit.

"Discover the words that endure. The lessons that uplift. The wisdom that never fades."

**Collect all three in
The Trilogy of Timeless Wisdom:**

Reflections • Revelations • Resolutions

– available wherever inspiring books are found –

About the Author

C.J. is the author of many inspirational books. An educator by profession, she has received numerous awards for her writing achievements. She is featured in Who's Who Among American Teachers and, as an entrepreneur, she was honored with the International and Business Career Award, C.J. has been recognized by the New York Assembly with a "Woman of Distinction" citation, as well as being selected as one of The Empowered Women of Queens, New York.

C.J. is a certified life coach and a personal consultant specializing in pageantry. As a multi-time, state and national queen, herself, she understands the importance of style and fostering a positive self-image. With over forty years of experience in the pageant arena, C.J. brings a wealth of knowledge and expertise to her work.

Beyond her professional accomplishments, C.J. is deeply involved in her community. She participates in bereavement groups, offering support to those dealing with grief. As a philanthropist, she devotes her time, talents, and resources to various charitable causes. Her artwork has been used to raise funds for churches and events, and she has donated proceeds from her book sales to those in need.

C.J's mission is rooted in service, bringing smiles, hope, and joy to those who need it most. She firmly believes that life's greatest rewards come from giving to others. For her, the most meaningful accomplishments transcend financial success and lie in the positive impact made on the lives of others.